The Natural World
AFRICA

Megan Cuthbert

www.av2books.com

AV² provides enriched content that supplements and complements this book. Weigl's AV² books strive to create inspired learning and engage young minds in a total learning experience.

Your AV² Media Enhanced books come alive with...

Audio
Listen to sections of the book read aloud.

Key Words
Study vocabulary, and complete a matching word activity.

Video
Watch informative video clips.

Quizzes
Test your knowledge.

Go to **www.av2books.com**, and enter this book's unique code.

BOOK CODE

F512120

Embedded Weblinks
Gain additional information for research.

Slide Show
View images and captions, and prepare a presentation.

AV² by Weigl brings you media enhanced books that support active learning.

Try This!
Complete activities and hands-on experiments.

... and much, much more!

Published by AV² by Weigl
350 5th Avenue, 59th Floor
New York, NY 10118
Websites: www.av2books.com   www.weigl.com

Library of Congress Cataloging-in-Publication Data

Cuthbert, Megan, author.
 Africa / Megan Cuthbert.
   pages cm. -- (The natural world)
 Summary: "Africa lies south of Europe, surrounded by the Atlantic, Indian, and Southern Oceans. The landscape of Africa ranges from rainforests to deserts. Learn more about this exciting environment in Africa. This is an AV2 media enhanced book. A unique book code printed on page 2 unlocks multimedia content. This book comes alive with video, audio, weblinks, slide shows, activities, hands-on experiments, and much more."-- Provided by publisher.
 Includes index.
 ISBN 978-1-4896-0934-2 (hardcover : alk. paper) -- ISBN 978-1-4896-0935-9 (softcover : alk. paper) --
ISBN 978-1-4896-0936-6 (single user ebk) -- ISBN 978-1-4896-0937-3 (multi user ebk)
 1. Natural history--Africa--Juvenile literature. 2. Ecology--Africa--Juvenile literature. 3. Africa--Environmental conditions--Juvenile literature. I. Title.
 QH194.C88 2014
 578.096--dc23
                                    2014004612

Printed in the United States of America in North Mankato, Minnesota
1 2 3 4 5 6 7 8 9 0 18 17 16 15 14

042014
WEP150314

Editor: Heather Kissock
Design: Mandy Christiansen

Every reasonable effort has been made to trace ownership and to obtain permission to reprint copyright material. The publishers would be pleased to have any errors or omissions brought to their attention so that they may be corrected in subsequent printings.

Weigl acknowledges Getty Images and Alamy as its primary image suppliers for this title.

Contents

Welcome to Africa!

Africa is the second largest continent in the world, covering an area of more than 11,000,000 square miles (28,489,869 square kilometers). The landscape ranges from rainforests to deserts. The Sahara Desert runs along the northern part of the continent and is the largest desert in the world. It covers one quarter of Africa's land area. Central Africa is home to the second largest rainforest in the world, the Congo rainforest.

The many African landscapes contain a huge range of plant and animal life. Many people travel to Africa to see the "Big Five." These are the five most popular animals on the continent. They are the lion, African elephant, Cape buffalo, leopard, and rhinoceros. Africa has more than 1,200 **species** of **mammals**, 2,000 bird species, and 100,000 types of insects and spiders. The variety of landscapes, plants, and animals are what make Africa a unique and varied continent.

Africa is home to **950** species of amphibians.

Hippos eat about

80
pounds
(36 kg) of plants per day.

40,000 to 60,000 plant species grow in Africa.

No two zebras have the exact same stripe pattern.

The African elephant lives in the southern part of the continent. It is the largest land animal in the world.

Unique African Life

Africa has a diverse range of plants, insects, animals, and birds. Some of these species are only found on the African continent. These are called endemic species. Endemic species are plants and animals that are found only in a certain region. Sometimes, endemic species are found throughout the continent. Other times, they are only found in a very small area. Often, species become endemic to one region because their **habitat** has been destroyed in other areas.

Gorillas are found in the lush, wet forests of West and Central Africa.

The island of Madagascar, which is off the east coast of Africa, is known for its large quantity of unique species. Madagascar separated from the rest of the African continent more than 160 million years ago. Since the island became separate from the mainland long ago, many unique plant and animal species developed on the island over time. Other areas in Africa, such as the Albertine Rift near the eastern coast and the Cape Floral Region at the southern tip of the continent, also have a large number of endemic species.

Madagascar

Madagascar is known for its rich diversity of plant and animal life. Of the island's 8,500 plant species, about 85 percent are unique. It also has 115 unique bird species. Many mammal species are also only found in Madagascar.

Africa

Madagascar

Madagascar is home to 67 unique mammal species.

Some Madagascar lemurs can leap up to **25 feet** *(7.6 meters).*

Chameleons can rotate each eye separately.

142 amphibian species are unique to Madagascar.

80% **of Madagascar's animals are endemic.**

A comet moth's tail can be up to 8 inches long (20 centimeters).

Where in the World?

Africa lies south of Europe, surrounded by the Atlantic, Indian, and Southern Oceans. The **equator** runs almost straight across the center of the continent. Places along the equator tend to receive the same amount of heat from the Sun all year round. This means that the temperatures near the equator are normally warm and do not change as much as areas that are farther away. Areas near the equator also tend to have more rainfall. Temperature and rainfall affect the types of plants that can grow. The rainfall, temperature, and plant life in an area also determine the types of animals that can live in the region.

ARCTIC OCEAN

ASIA

EUROPE

ATLANTIC OCEAN

AFRICA

INDIAN OCEAN

EQUATOR

SOUTHERN OCEAN

African Biomes

Areas that have similar temperatures, rainfall, and types of plants and animals are called biomes. Similar biomes are found throughout the world. Africa has four types of land biomes. They are grassland, desert, rainforest, and chaparral. These biomes are found in areas of the continent that have similar climates.

The Kalahari Desert in Africa's southeast is one of nine deserts on the continent.

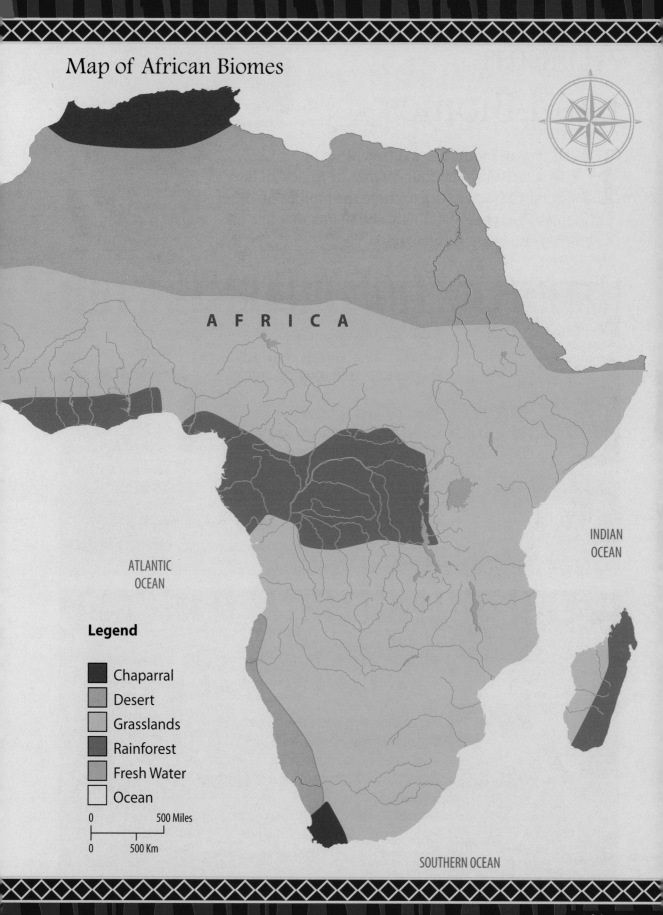

Map of African Biomes

A F R I C A

ATLANTIC
OCEAN

INDIAN
OCEAN

Legend

- Chaparral
- Desert
- Grasslands
- Rainforest
- Fresh Water
- Ocean

0   500 Miles

0   500 Km

SOUTHERN OCEAN

African Land Biomes

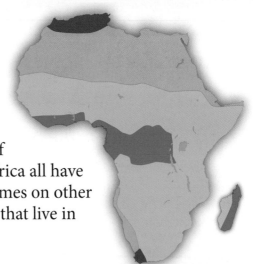

Each type of biome has a different set of characteristics. The four biomes in Africa all have similar characteristics to the same biomes on other continents. The types of animals and plants that live in the biomes also share similar traits.

Grasslands

Grasslands are open grass-covered plains. They are often called savannas in Africa.

Plants: Grasslands feature different grass species, short trees and shrubs. Grass species include Rhodes grass, lemon grass, and Bermuda grass. Baobab and acacia trees also grow here.

Animals: Large herds of grazing animals, such as zebras, wildebeest, and giraffes, live in grasslands. These animals are **prey** for **carnivores**, such as lions, hyenas, and cheetahs.

Winter
68 to 78°F
(20 to 26°C)
Summer
78 to 86°F
(26 to 30°C)

Rainy Season
15 to 25"
(38 to 64 cm)
Dry Season
Less than **2 inches**
(5 cm)

Desert

The desert biome receives very little rain. It is hot during the day and cool at night.

Plants: Desert biomes have very few plants. For the most part, plant life consists of a few shrubs and short trees scattered throughout the desert. These plants tend to store water in their stems and have deep roots.

Animals: Most animals in deserts are nocturnal and burrow underground to avoid the heat. African desert animals include meerkats, camels, and horned toads.

Daytime Average
100°F (38°C)
Nighttime Average
50°F (10°C)

Less than 10" (25 cm) per year

The exact species that live in a biome are different for each continent and region within the continent. For example, a desert biome is home to snakes that can live in dry heat. However, the exact species of snake that lives in the Sahara Desert might be different from a species that lives in the Kalahari desert.

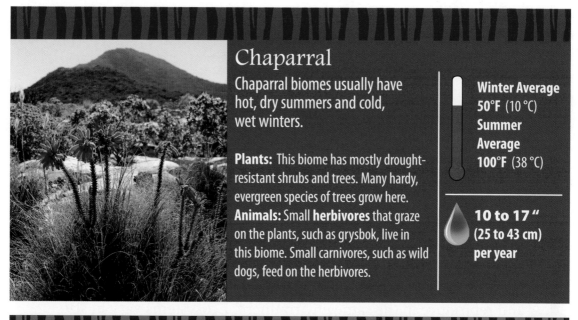

Chaparral

Chaparral biomes usually have hot, dry summers and cold, wet winters.

Plants: This biome has mostly drought-resistant shrubs and trees. Many hardy, evergreen species of trees grow here.
Animals: Small **herbivores** that graze on the plants, such as grysbok, live in this biome. Small carnivores, such as wild dogs, feed on the herbivores.

Winter Average 50°F (10 °C)
Summer Average 100°F (38 °C)

10 to 17" **(25 to 43 cm) per year**

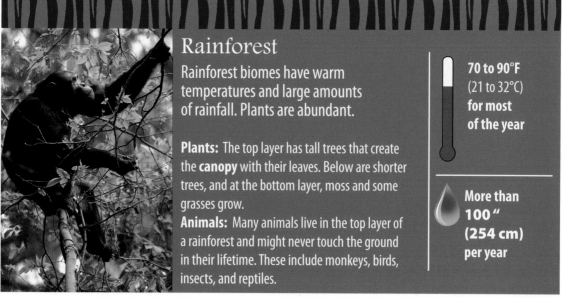

Rainforest

Rainforest biomes have warm temperatures and large amounts of rainfall. Plants are abundant.

Plants: The top layer has tall trees that create the **canopy** with their leaves. Below are shorter trees, and at the bottom layer, moss and some grasses grow.
Animals: Many animals live in the top layer of a rainforest and might never touch the ground in their lifetime. These include monkeys, birds, insects, and reptiles.

70 to 90°F (21 to 32°C) **for most of the year**

More than 100" **(254 cm) per year**

African Ecosystems and Habitats

Every biome is made up of many different ecosystems. Ecosystems are communities of plants, animals, and other living things that live, feed, and reproduce in the same environment. Ecosystems vary in size. They can be as small as a single tree or as large as a forest. The living things in an ecosystem interact with each other, relying on each other and their environment for food and shelter.

Within every ecosystem is one or more habitats. A habitat supplies the needs of a plant or animal, providing it with food, water, oxygen, and an appropriate climate. The ecosystems found within a biome are very diverse, as are habitats within ecosystems. Africa has many distinct and well-known ecosystems and habitats.

The Serengeti Plains near the eastern coast are one of Africa's best-known habitats. The Serengeti is part of a grassland biome. Zebras, giraffes, and other hooved animals live on the Serengeti and graze on the grass. Many carnivores, such as lions, live on the plains and hunt the grazing animals.

Approximately 5 million square miles (13 million sq. km) of savanna cover the African continent.

The Sahara Desert is more than 3.6 million square miles (9.3 million sq. km) in size. Very little plant life grows in the desert, except cacti and shrubs. Herbivores such as the desert beetle, live in the desert and feed on these plants.

The Congo rainforest in central Africa has one of the tallest rainforest tree species, the kapok tree. Trees in the rainforest are home to animals such as chimpanzees and sloths.

The Western Cape province in the south of Africa is part of the chaparral biome. Fynbos, or fine bush, are evergreen shrubs that are found throughout the area. Larger mammals, such as the klipspringer, feed on the fynbos.

Giraffes live in grasslands that have plenty of trees. Giraffes use their long necks to eat leaves from the treetops.

Plant Life in Africa

Africa's plant life has **adapted** features to suit the conditions of its habitat. The hot and dry chaparral regions of Africa are mostly covered in shrubs and small trees that require very little water. Most plants and trees found in the grasslands are fire-resistant, since the dry, flat grasslands often experience seasonal fires. The rainfall and warm temperatures of the African rainforest sustain a range of plant life. There are about 600 different tree species in the rainforest. Vegetation is limited in the desert. Desert plants have adapted large root systems to help them absorb more water.

The king protea is just one of the 2,000 species of protea plants found in Africa.

King Protea

The king protea grows well in the dry chaparral areas of Africa. The plant has a long stem and thick, stiff leaves that make it look similar to an artichoke. The king protea is able to take in moisture through its leaves, which helps in the dry regions where it grows. When it blooms, the flower of the protea can be up to 12 inches (30.5 cm) wide.

Red Oat Grass

Red oat grass is the most common grass species found in the African grasslands. It grows between 1 and 6 feet (31 and 183 cm) tall. The grass changes color from green to orange-brown in the summer. Red oat grass can survive fires because its seeds are buried deep underground.

Red oat grass makes up 16 percent of East Africa's grasslands.

Mahogany Tree

The African mahogany tree is one of the trees that form the canopy in the rainforest. The tree grows up to 98 feet (30 m) in height. It has a smooth, thick trunk covered in a dark gray bark. The trunk can grow to be 6 feet (1.8 m) in diameter.

The leaves on the mahogany tree are glossy and grow thickly together.

Welwitschia Mirabilis

The welwitschia mirabilis is one of the most unique plants found in Africa's Namib Desert. The plant has two large strap-like leaves that grow along the desert ground. These broad, flat leaves keep the soil underneath cool and moist. The welwitschia survives well in its desert environment. Some plants are more than 1,500 years old.

Welwitschia is only found in part of the Namibia desert on the southwest coast of the continent.

Just the Facts

The Congo rainforest has more than 11,000 species of plants.

More than 2,500 species of vines grow in the African rainforest.

The king protea is the national flower of South Africa.

More than 400 species of plants have been identified in the Kalahari Desert.

Baobab trees store up to 31,700 gallons (120,000 litres) of water in their trunk.

Insects, Reptiles and Amphibians

Stick insects, grasshoppers, dung beetles, termites, and mosquitoes are just some of the more than 100,000 species of insects in Africa. Insects are common prey for many reptiles and amphibians. Lizards, skinks, tortoises, and frogs are abundant and come in a variety of shapes and sizes. There are 400 species of snakes in Africa. Many of the features that make these insects, reptiles, and amphibians unique also help them to survive in their ecosystems.

Worker termites are cream-colored. They build tunnels and gather food for other termites.

Termites

There are more than 1,000 termite species in Africa. Plants and dead wood are the main food source for termites. Termites live underground or build large mounds. The structure of these mounds allows air to flow through, keeping them cool inside.

Horned Viper

The horned viper is pale and sand-colored. Its coloring helps the snake blend with the sand it burrows into in the deserts of Africa. Burrowing protects the viper from the heat and gives it a hiding place to catch its prey. The horned viper is named for two spine-like scales that protrude above each eye.

Horned vipers often move their bodies in front of their head. This helps block the Sun's rays from their face.

Jackson's Chameleon

Jackson's chameleon is found in the rainforests of Africa. It is green in color and can grow up to 12 inches (30.5 cm) in length. A fully-grown male has three horns on the front of its head. Jackson's chameleons eat ants, butterflies, snails, worms, and other small reptiles. They will also eat leaves and berries.

Chameleons have five toes on each foot, three pointing outward and two pointing inward. This helps them grip onto branches.

Geometric Tortoise

The geometric tortoise is one of the rarest tortoise species in the world. It is found in the fynbos of southern Africa. This small tortoise has a black and yellow geometric pattern on its shell. It feeds on leaves, flowers, and grass.

The geometric tortoise is very rare. There are only about 3,000 geometric tortoises in nature.

Just the Facts

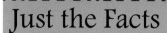

African rock pythons can eat animals as large as **antelopes** and **crocodiles**.

The giant African millipede is the largest millipede species.

Africa has more than **1,600 species of bees.**

There are 5 species of poisonous spiders in Africa.

The African giant swallowtail is the largest butterfly in the world.

Birds and Mammals

Africa has become known for its distinct mammal species. The continent has 90 species of antelope, as well as other hooved mammal species such as zebra, giraffe, hippopotamus, elephant, and rhinoceros. Three of the world's great apes species, the chimpanzee, bonobos, and gorilla, live in Africa's rainforests. Lions, leopards, and cheetahs are some of the more than 60 carnivore species found on the continent. Some carnivores, such as the jackal, will feed on the meat left over from other carnivores. These **predators** and **scavengers** play an important role in their environments, often preying on weak and sick animals. Africa also has approximately 2,300 species of birds.

Secretary birds were named for the feathers behind their head. The feathers look like the quill pens secretaries used to tuck behind their ears.

Secretary Bird

The secretary bird stands at more than 4 feet (1.2 m) tall, with long legs that help it walk through the African grasslands, searching for food. Along with its long legs, the bird is known for the long dark quills that stick out from the back of its head. Although it normally travels on foot, the secretary bird can fly, and will nest and roost in trees at night.

Jerboa

The mouse-like jerboa lives in the desert regions of Africa. It grows between 2 and 6 inches (5 and 15 cm) in length, with a tail that is longer than its body. The jerboa uses its tail for balance. It hops much like a kangaroo. The jerboa survives in the dry, hot desert by burrowing underground during the day and feeding on desert plants at night.

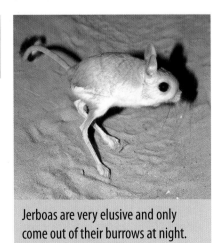

Jerboas are very elusive and only come out of their burrows at night.

Klipspringer

The klipspringer is one of the smallest species of antelopes. It lives in the rocky terrain found in Africa's chaparral areas. The klipspringer is dull brown or gray in color. This helps it blend in with rocks and hides it from predators. The klipspringer feeds on evergreen shrubs, grass, and flowers.

The klipspringer has a heavy body and short legs to help it navigate through its rocky habitat.

Black-and-White Colobus Monkey

The black-and-white colobus monkey spends almost all of its life in the branches of the African rainforest. It feeds on fruit, seeds, flowers, and bark from the trees. The species is mostly black, with a white strip running down its back and tail. The black-and-white colobus monkey is the only species of monkey that does not have thumbs.

Black-and-white colobus monkeys can leap up to 50 feet (15 m).

Just the Facts

Zzz...
Lions sleep for
20 hours
a day.

Gorillas are considered the most intelligent animal, after humans.

Aardvarks eat mostly **termites.**

Ostriches can sprint more than 40 miles (64 km) **per hour.**

4 of the world's fastest land mammals live in Africa—the cheetah, wildebeest, lion, and Thomson's gazelle.

African Aquatic Biomes

Besides the different land biomes, Africa also has aquatic biomes. The two main types of aquatic biome are freshwater and marine. The main factor that separates these two biomes is the amount of salt contained in the water.

Aquatic Ecosystems and Habitats

Aquatic biomes contain many different ecosystems and habitats that support plant and animal life. There are many large freshwater lakes near the eastern coast, known as the African Great Lakes. The largest of these is Lake Victoria. It is the second largest freshwater lake in the world. The Nile River is the longest river in the world. It flows north from inland northeastern Africa. The Nile River is more than 4,000 miles (6,437 km) long.

Marine Biome

Oceans and **coral reefs** are part of Africa's marine biome. Coral reefs are found in the ocean, but have different water conditions.

Oceans are the largest part of the marine biome. Ocean water that is closer to the surface receives more sunlight and is warmer than deeper areas of the ocean. Coral reefs are found in warm, shallow water.

Plants: Marine algae, kelp, and seaweed all grow in Africa's marine biome.

About 3% salt content

Animals: Sea turtles, fish, sharks, stingrays, whales, seals, and dolphins are just some of the animals that live in the oceans surrounding Africa.

The three oceans that surround Africa make up most of Africa's marine biome. Due to their size, oceans contain a large variety of ecosystems. The depth of the water affects the water temperature and the amount of sunlight that filters through. This affects the types of life that can thrive in those areas. Africa's coral reefs are found along the eastern and southern coasts of the continent. Coral is the dominant organism. However, many species of plants, fish, **mollusks**, turtles, and sharks live in and around the reefs.

The Okavango delta is part of the freshwater biome. It is a large wetland formed by the Okavango River.

Freshwater Biome

Africa's freshwater biomes include ponds, lakes, streams, rivers, and wetlands. Each of these has different water conditions.

Water in lakes is usually constant and contains many **nutrients**. The flow of water in rivers affects the type of life in these ecosystems. The amount of water found in wetlands is based on factors such as rainfall and time of year.

Plants: Algae, reeds, grasses, and water lilies can be found in Africa's freshwater biomes.

Less than 1% salt content

Animals: Fish, plankton, snails, turtles, and crocodiles are a few of the animals living in and around Africa's fresh waters.

African Aquatic Life

Factors such as temperature, nutrients, and oxygen in the water affect the life that grows in freshwater and marine biomes. The main form of plant life is algae. Different algae species have adapted to live in either freshwater or saltwater biomes. Fish species are also divided into freshwater or saltwater varieties. Some birds, such as flamingos, and mammals, such as hippopotamuses, spend most of their day in freshwater lakes. Large marine mammals, such as dugongs, whales, and dolphins, live underwater, but must surface to breathe.

Lesser flamingos travel in large groups. Some flocks contain more than 1 million flamingos.

Lesser Flamingos

Lesser flamingos are usually found in large flocks in the freshwater lakes of Africa's Rift Valley. These flamingos spend their time in shallow waters eating blue-green algae and small mollusks. Three quarters of the world's population of lesser flamingos live in east Africa. Although they mostly stand in the waters, the birds are also good swimmers.

Nile Crocodile

Africa's largest crocodile, the Nile crocodile, lives in rivers, freshwater marshes, and swamps. The crocodile grows to about 16 feet (5 m) in length and 500 pounds (227 kg) in weight. It feeds mainly on fish. If given the opportunity, the crocodile will also prey on larger animals, such as zebra, birds, and small hippopotamuses.

The Nile crocodile has more than 60 teeth. If one tooth falls out, a new tooth will grow in to replace it.

Dugong

The dugong is a large marine mammal that lives in the ocean off the eastern coast of Africa. The dugong grows up to 9.8 feet (3 m) in length. It has a large snout, paddle-like front flippers, and a tail like a whale. Dugongs feed on underwater marine grasses. They can only hold their breath for 6 minutes before they have to surface for air.

The dugong uses its bristled, rough upper lip to rip the grass from the ocean floor.

Whale Shark

The giant whale shark is found in the ocean waters around Africa. At about 40 feet (12 m) long, it is the largest fish in the world. The whale shark has an impressive 5-foot (152-cm) wide mouth, but only uses it to eat large amounts of plankton that grow in the water.

A whale shark can weigh up to 26,000 pounds (11,800 kilograms).

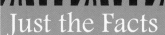

Just the Facts

10,000+
species of marine plants and animals can be found around the southern coast of Africa.

Nile crocodiles will attack large animals such as giraffes, lions, and buffalo.

The world's largest turtle, the leatherback, nests along the coasts of west Africa.

Marine algae are the largest producer of oxygen in the world.

1938
The year the first live coelacanth was found off the south coast of Africa

Maintaining Balance

There is a complex balance in any ecosystem. The temperature and rainfall in an ecosystem affects the species of plants that grow there. The types of plants that grow affect the types of insects, reptiles, and amphibians that live in an area, which also often determines the species of birds and mammals that live in the area. This is why diversity is so important in Africa. If a continent has many different ecosystems, it can support many varieties of plant life. This plant life then supports a variety of herbivores, which in turn provides variety for different species of carnivores. When there is a large diversity of species in one part of an ecosystem, it creates variety in other areas.

Introducing New Species

When a new or non-native species is introduced to an ecosystem, it has a major impact on the organisms living there. The different African species have adapted over time to suit their place in the ecosystem. When a non-native species is introduced, it often has no natural predators. The foreign species will start to overtake the ecosystem because there is nothing to keep it in balance. The water hyacinth, originally from South America, was introduced in Africa in the 1800s. The flower grows on the tops of freshwater lakes. It has been causing major damage to many habitats, including Lake Victoria. Here, the flower

Hippopotamuses can spread vegetation, including non-native species such as water hyacinth, in ponds and lakes.

grows quickly, covering the lake and removing sunlight and oxygen from the water. This has led to many fish species choking from lack of oxygen levels in the water.

Ecosystem Interactions

All organisms in an ecosystem interact with each other. They are each part of a food chain. Every food chain contains producers, primary and secondary consumers, and decomposers. Producers are plants that use the Sun's energy to make food. Primary consumers are herbivores that eat plants. Secondary consumers feed on the herbivores. Decomposers break down dead organisms and return nutrients to the soil. Some plants and animals also provide shelter for other organisms.

Aardvarks
Aardvarks dig holes searching for their main food source, termites. These holes are used by warthogs for shelter.

Cheetahs
Cheetahs are secondary consumers. They feed on warthogs, aardvarks, and other small animals. Cheetahs take shelter from the Sun under acacia trees.

Warthogs
Warthogs are primary consumers. They feed on red oat grass and other plants. They are hunted by carnivores in the savanna.

Termites
Termites are decomposers. They feed on dead trees and plant matter, such as red oat grass and acacia trees. They also provide food for aardvarks.

Red Oat Grass and Acacia Trees
Red oat grass and acacia trees are producers. They provide food for termites and warthogs. Acacia trees provides shelter for many animals, including cheetahs.

Diversity for Humans

The diversity of African ecosystems has positive effects for humans. African plants and animals have long been an important source of food and shelter for Africans. They continue to be an important resource, benefitting people around the world. Africa is the source of many food crops. About 7,000 of Africa's plant species are used for food. Each plant contains different vitamins and nutrients.

Plants play an important role in medicine. Many African species are used in **traditional medicine**. **Pharmaceutical** companies also use African plant species in the creation of different drugs. Scientists continue to research the ability of different African plant species to treat diseases such as cancer.

Many people visit African countries to view the diverse wildlife. This nature-based tourism brings money to local and national governments.

Human Impact

The human demand for plant and animal resources has become a threat to the habitats of many African species. In order to produce higher amounts of resources, large areas of natural areas have been destroyed to create more room for agriculture and human living. When African habitats, such as savannas, shrink in size, the animal populations decrease as well. In the past 50 years, the lion population of Africa has gone from 100,000 to 35,000. When habitats are completely destroyed, many of the species that depend on that habitat die as well.

More than 500,000 trees are cut down every year in the western regions of the Congo rainforest. The wood is used mainly for construction.

Conserving Nature

There are many ways that governments, groups, and individuals are working toward conserving Africa's ecosystems. Africa has a total protected land area of more than 7.7 million square miles (2 million sq. km). This land is spread throughout the continent in more than 3,000 separate protected areas. Some of these protected areas are **game reserves** and national parks. Private reserves are owned and managed by individuals or groups. These areas are designed to help conserve the local plant and animal life. Many game reserves are open to the public so that people can view the wildlife in their natural habitat. Africa has 198 marine areas that are also under protection. These areas are carefully monitored to make sure the balance of life within each ecosystem remains stable. By working to conserve these areas, some of Africa's diverse life forms and landscapes can also be preserved.

Savannas are one of the most commonly protected land areas in Africa.

Make an Ecosystem Web

Use this book, and research on the Internet, to create an African ecosystem.

1. Find an African plant or animal. Think about what habitat it lives in.
2. Find at least three organisms that are found in the same habitat. This could include plants, insects, amphibians, reptiles, birds, and mammals.
3. How do these species interact with each other? Do they provide food or shelter for the other organisms?
4. Begin linking these organisms together to show which organisms rely on each other for food or shelter.
5. Once your ecosystem web is complete, think about how removing one organism would affect the other organisms in the web.

African Ecosystem

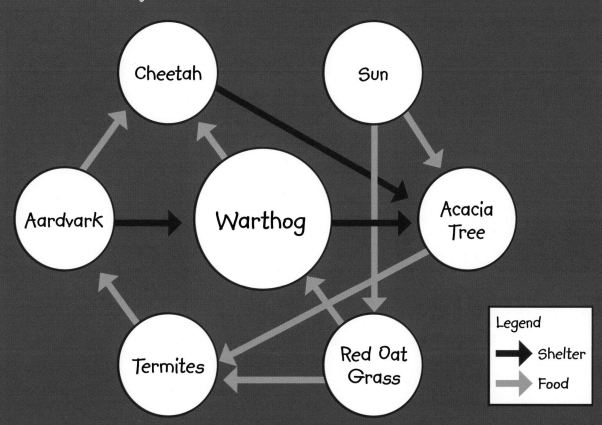

Quiz

1 How many African plant species are used for food?

About 7,000

2 How many species of snake live in Africa?

400

3 In which direction does the Nile River flow?

North

4 What is the name of the second largest rainforest in the world?

The Congo rainforest

5 What animals make up the "Big Five"?

Lion, African elephant, Cape buffalo, leopard, and rhinoceros

6 How many mammal species are endemic to Madagascar?

67

7 How many African marine areas are under protection?

198

8 Which South American plant was introduced to Africa in the late 1800s?

The water hyacinth

9 To which biome does the Serengeti belong?

The grassland biome

10 What is the key difference between freshwater and marine biomes?

The salt content

Key Words

adapted: changed to suit an environment

canopy: the layer of trees at the very top of the rainforest

carnivores: animals that eat other animals

coral reefs: underwater structures made up of calcium carbonate and populated by marine organisms

equator: an imaginary line drawn around Earth's center

game reserves: areas set aside for animal conservation

habitat: an environment that is occupied by a particular species of plant, animal, or other kind of organism

herbivores: animals that rely on vegetation for food

mammals: animals that have hair or fur and give birth to live young

mollusks: soft-bodied invertebrates, such as snails, slugs, or octopuses

nutrients: substances that provide the nourishment essential for growth

pharmaceutical: relating to medicinal drugs

predators: animals that hunt other animals for food

prey: animals that are hunted for food

scavengers: animals that feed on the dead remains of other animals or plants

species: a group of organisms that share similar characteristics

traditional medicine: any system of healthcare that has ancient roots

Index

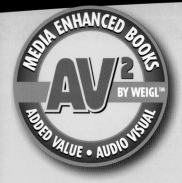

Log on to www.av2books.com

AV² by Weigl brings you media enhanced books that support active learning. Go to www.av2books.com, and enter the special code found on page 2 of this book. You will gain access to enriched and enhanced content that supplements and complements this book. Content includes video, audio, weblinks, quizzes, a slide show, and activities.

AV² Online Navigation

Audio
Listen to sections of the book read aloud.

Book Pages
AV² pages directly correspond to pages in the book.

Video
Watch informative video clips.

Key Words
Study vocabulary, and complete a matching word activity.

Embedded Weblinks
Gain additional information for research.

Try This!
Complete activities and hands-on experiments.

Quizzes
Test your knowledge.

Slide Show
View images and captions, and prepare a presentation.

AV² was built to bridge the gap between print and digital. We encourage you to tell us what you like and what you want to see in the future.

Sign up to be an AV² Ambassador at www.av2books.com/ambassador.

Due to the dynamic nature of the Internet, some of the URLs and activities provided as part of AV² by Weigl may have changed or ceased to exist. AV² by Weigl accepts no responsibility for any such changes. All media enhanced books are regularly monitored to update addresses and sites in a timely manner. Contact AV² by Weigl at 1-866-649-3445 or av2books@weigl.com with any questions, comments, or feedback.